frog throat

by Martin Waddell
Illustrated by
Trevor Dunton

Baby Giraffe was out eating leaves. He gobbled and gobbled and gobbled then ...

Oooooooop!
Baby Giraffe almost choked and …

Gulp! Gulp! Gulp!
He shivered and shook,

and he ran to his mother.

5

"There's a frog in my throat!"
gasped Baby Giraffe.
"There's a frog in my throat,
and it's tickling
like mad!"
"Don't be silly!"
said Mother Giraffe.

"But there is!"
gurgled Baby.

"Just open up wide!"
said Mother Giraffe,
and when Baby did,
she looked down inside.

7

Down ...
... down ... down ...
down ... Down deep inside
she saw eyes

– bright shiny frog eyes
looking up!

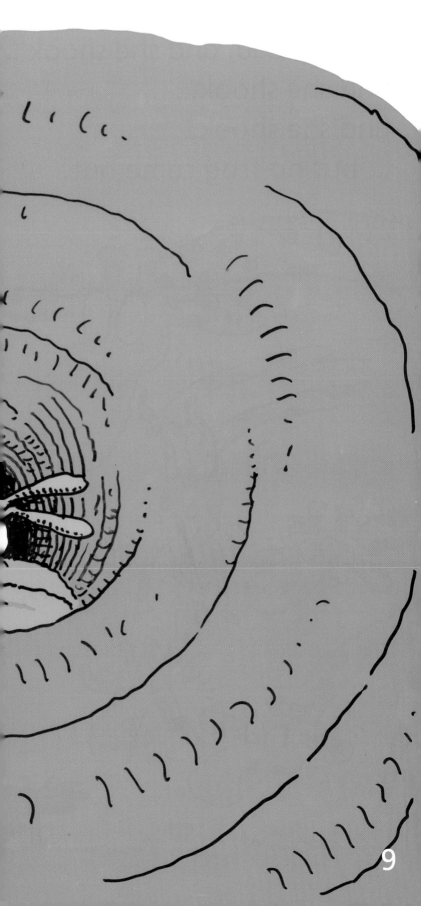

"Oh my!" said
Mother Giraffe.
Then she stood Baby Giraffe
on his head, and she shook ..
and she shook...
and she shook...
... but no frog came out.

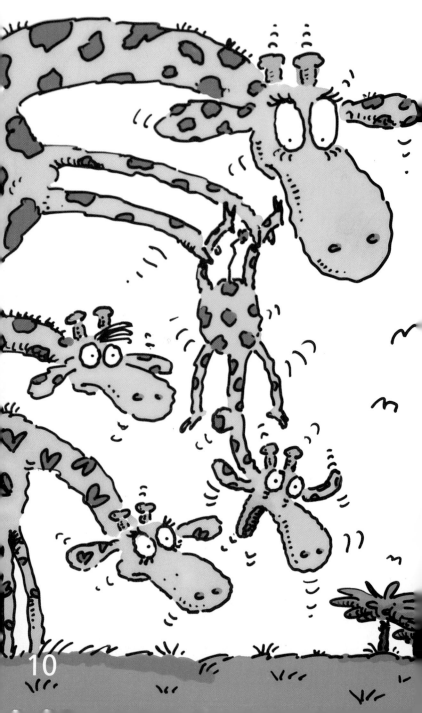

"Bang Baby's back!" said
Baby's Big Sister.
Bang! Bang! Bang! Bang!
... but no frog came out.

"Spin Baby about, and the frog will come out!" said Baby's Big Brother. And they whizzed Baby round with his head on the ground ...

... but no frog came out.

"I feel really sick!" groaned Baby Giraffe going green. "Oh good!" said the others. They waited and hoped ...

... but no frog came out.

Then a little frog appeared on a leaf by the ear of the biggest Giraffe.

"Pardon me," said the
little frog.
"I'm sure it's just a mistake,
but one of you's swallowed
my Auntie."

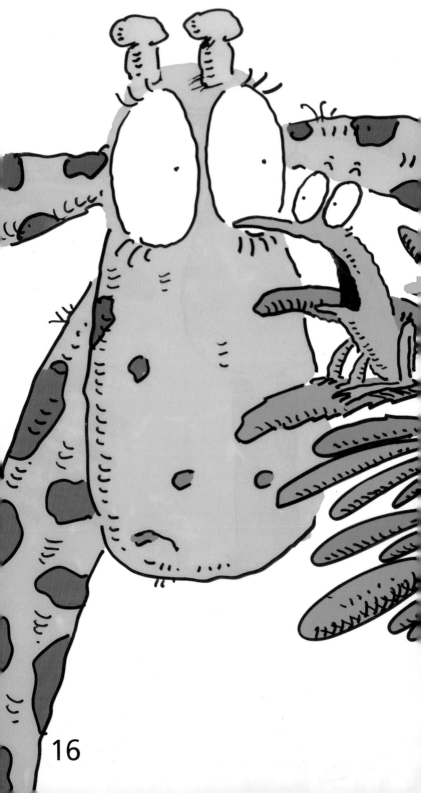

The little frog was really upset, and so ...

... down ...

... down ...

... down ...

... down ...

... below was his Auntie.

17

The Wisest Giraffe
was having a drink
by the pool when
he heard the fuss,
and came
over to help.

"A frog in the throat?" said the Wisest Giraffe.
"Just make Baby laugh!"

They laid Baby down by the
side of the pool,
with his neck sticking out
over the water.

"Now watch me," said the Wisest Giraffe,
and he tickled the throat of Baby Giraffe with his tail.

This made Baby laugh
Ha-Ha-Ha-Ha!
... and made the frog hop
in his throat!

Hop ...

   ... hop ...

      ... hop ...

         ... hop!

            ... Plop!

"That's how to cope with a frog in the throat!" said the Wisest Giraffe.